WHY WE MUST PROTEST

E VARATHKANTH

XpressPublishing
An imprint of Notion Press

Old No. 38, New No. 6
McNichols Road, Chetpet
Chennai - 600 031

First Published by Notion Press 2020
Copyright © E Varathkanth 2020
All Rights Reserved.

ISBN 978-1-64805-112-8

Contents

CHAPTER I

Introduction

'Protest' is a strong word. To protest is to have a strong feeling about an issue and to act on the feeling.

In the India of 2020, protesting a government is routinely branded as anti-national. If you protest, you will face a barrage of questions:

- Why are you protesting an elected government? Aren't we in a democracy?
- Why are you protesting Acts duly passed by the Parliament?
- Instead of protesting on the streets, why don't you challenge the government in Court?
- Why do you protest after the highest Courts of the land have decided the issue in favour of the government?
- Why do you protest without police permission?
- Why do you raise slogans of Azaadi (freedom)?
- Why didn't you protest a similar issue earlier?

But our country pioneered the use of non-violent protest to gain freedom from a colonial power barely 70 years ago. Given this history, is it right to denounce protesters in today's India?

This book is an answer to that question.

CHAPTER II

Protests in India before Independence

Dandi March, 1930

The Indian National Congress adopted the objective of complete self-rule in its Lahore session in December 1929. It was decided to launch a civil disobedience movement across the country. Mahatma Gandhi decided to launch the first such movement against Salt tax imposed by the British government. He led a march spanning 384 kilometres over 24 days to Dandi where he disobeyed the law by making salt. It sparked similar civil disobedience against the salt tax by millions of Indians.

Gandhi deliberately picked salt tax as the first subject of national civil disobedience movement. Salt was a universal daily use item and resonated with a large section of Indians. Additionally, salt tax contributed to 8% of the British Raj tax revenue. Why must Salt Tax be paid by millions of poor Indians to the British Raj? The extreme immorality of this tax made it a powerful target for Gandhi's protest.

Gandhi's Dandi March led to a mass civil disobedience movement with millions breaking the Salt laws. The British government arrested over 60,000 people within a month.

While the Salt Satyagraha did not immediately result in concrete concessions from the British, Jawaharlal Nehru believed that it shook the British government machinery and brought a lasting change in the attitude of Indians. American civil rights activist Martin Luther King Jr has also cited Satyagraha and Dandi March, in particular, as a strong influence in his fight for civil rights for African Americans in the 1960s.

• • •

Vaikom Satyagraha, 1924-25

Historically, India's caste system demanded that dalits (members of oppressed castes) should not enter temples or the roads adjacent to temples. In 1865, the Government of Travancore notified that all public roads in the state were open to all castes. This was however not implemented due to social pressure. Several years later, the High Court of Travancore ruled that the Government notification will not apply to all roads. Consequently, by law, the roads around the Shiva temple in Vaikom were not open for dalits.

On 30th March 1924, the Kerala arm of the Indian National Congress launched a Satyagraha against this and several members courted arrest.

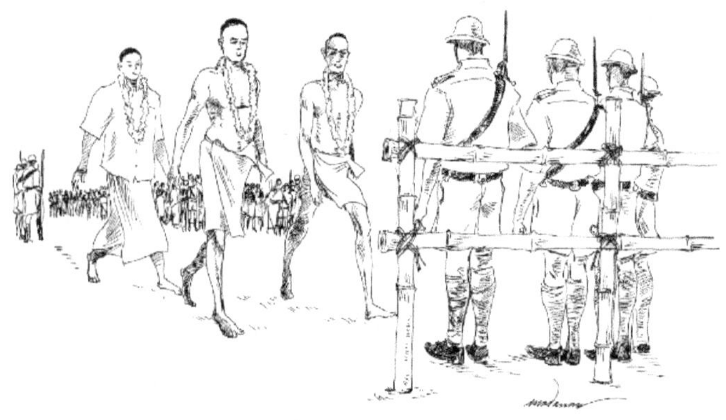

By 13th April, at the request of the Kerala members, Periyar arrived to lead the agitation. Periyar was then the President of Tamil Nadu's Congress arm. Over the course of several months, Periyar mobilized support for the protest in villages around Vaikom as well as towns in Kerala & Tamil Nadu. The Satyagraha ended in partial victory in November 1925 when 3 of the 4 streets were thrown open to members of all castes. After sustained pressure, in 1936, the new Maharaja of Travancore abolished the ban on dalits' entry into temples.

• • •

Mahad Satyagraha, 1927

The caste system prohibited dalits from accessing water in public tanks. In 1923, the Bombay Legislative Council passed a resolution that dalits must not be restricted from accessing places built and maintained by the government. In 1924, the Municipal Council of Mahad (part of the

Bombay province) passed a resolution to enforce the act. But social pressure prevented dalits from accessing water in public tanks. In 1927, the dalit champion Dr B.R. Ambedkar led a Satyagraha at Mahad to enable dalits' access of the public tank. Ambedkar led a Dalit march towards the public tank and drank water from the tank.

However, the Satyagraha did not result in immediate success. The oppressor castes conducted a 'purification ritual' at the tank and dalits were again denied access to the tank. In 1937, the Bombay High Court ruled in favour of the dalits.

Dr B.R. Ambedkar went on to lead the team that drafted our Indian Constitution after our Independence. The Constitution abolished untouchability. The Government of India has also passed laws punishing those who practise untouchability. However, the practice of caste discrimination continues in various forms. For example, in

2016, a temple priest in Uttar Pradesh attacked a 13-year old dalit girl for drawing water from the temple well.

• • •

The Indian Independence movement saw many such instances of peaceful protests. The three protests highlighted above were against unjust laws or non-implementation of just laws. And the protest form was rooted in Satyagraha.

Gandhi coined the term Satyagraha to denote determined but non-violent resistance to evil. Protesters adopting Satyagraha must first obtain a clear insight into the real nature of an evil situation by seeking truth in a spirit of peace and love. And then the protesters must refuse to submit to the wrong or cooperate with it in any way.

In other words, Gandhi saw Satyagraha as the right response in the face of evil - be it in the form of a government action or a societal practice.

After India gained Independence in 1947, did Satyagraha become irrelevant?

CHAPTER III

The relevance of Satyagraha

A democracy has several checks and balances. The people vote and decide their own representatives. Elected representatives in the legislature hold the executive accountable. The courts review the legality of a government's actions. And an independent media shines the light on deficiencies in the executive, legislature or judiciary. If citizens have a grievance with a government's actions, can they not depend on these checks and balances in the system?

Do they need the weapon of Satyagraha that Gandhi used against a colonial ruler? Here are four reasons the answer to this question is a resounding 'yes'.

1. The answer lies in the Preamble to our constitution. "We, the people of India, ... do give to ourselves this constitution." The entire Constitution is defined by us and for us. And it is not meant to limit our choices to only those mechanisms mentioned in the constitution. Further, independent media is not mentioned in the Constitution either, but it is widely regarded as a key component of our democracy. Similarly, civil society is entirely within its rights to make its case outside of these institutions.

2. The answer lies in the definition of Satyagraha. It is a weapon to fight evil. In a functioning democracy, checks and balances may make it difficult for the government

to do evil. But it is not impossible for the government to do evil. And as long as the government has the ability to do evil, the people have the right to resort to Satyagraha to counter it.

3. The answer lies in our history. In our short history as Independent India, we have seen a large number of protests on various issues. Until recently, very few (if any) of these protests were denounced as anti-national. A few examples: India Against Corruption protests of 2011-12, Jallikattu protests in Marina Beach in 2017, Telangana Statehood movement till 2014. A longer list of protests in Independent India is provided in the next chapter.

4. The answer lies in the independent history of the United States of America. Why speak of USA? The US has been an independent democratic republic for nearly 250 years now and has during this period, evolved its laws to make equality more universal. We will now highlight five landmark protests against the American government in the past century alone.

According to the segregation laws prevalent then, separate seating areas were provided in buses for white and black people. Rosa Parks defied these laws in 1955 and her arrest sparked a wave of protests against segregation laws. On the day of her trial, Black churches organized bus boycott movements. Most of the 40,000 black commuters walked instead of taking the bus, some as far as 30 kilometres. The boycott lasted for 381 days till the Supreme Court ruled segregation laws unconstitutional.

In 1965, African Americans marched from Selma to Montgomery to demonstrate their desire to exercise their constitutional right to vote. They were brutally assaulted by state troopers. This televised assault evoked national outrage and eventually lead to the passage of the Voting Rights Act 1965, which enabled universal voting rights. Incidentally, in the picture above, the person at the foreground being beaten by a cop is John Lewis. In 1986, he was elected to the lower house of the US Legislature and has been its member since then.

Even when the country was in a war with Vietnam, large number of US citizens demanded that their country end the war. The protests did not immediately end the war, but built enormous pressure on the government.

In February 2013, demonstrations were held in several cities in the US and around the world demanding that US should not enter into a war with Iraq. However, the war began a few weeks later.

The day after Donald Trump was sworn in as President, a large demonstration was conducted by women to highlight their opposition to Trump's anti-women statements. The march was not a sign of illegitimacy of a duly elected President, but it was instead a strong expression of dissent towards the President's nature in spite of his election win.

• • •

In the examples cited above, Americans demonstrated their right to protest unjust laws, acts of war and the nature of a newly elected President. In some instances, the injustices were later remedied. But nevertheless, the citizens were allowed to register their protest against perceived injustice.

We must emphatically conclude that Satyagraha continues to be relevant in a democracy.

"When injustice becomes law, resistance becomes duty."

CHAPTER IV

Protests in Independent India

Potti Sreeramulu was a freedom fighter and a member of Gandhi's Sabarmati Ashram. In 1952, he went on a fast demanding a separate Andhra state and died. Two weeks later, Prime Minister Jawaharlal Nehru announced the creation of an Andhra state.

In 1964, after Jawaharlal Nehru's death, there was concern in Tamil Nadu that the Central government may not honour Nehru's assurance that English will continue to be the Official Language. When the state government introduced a bill to implement Three Language Policy (English Tamil Hindi), it was condemned as a form of Hindi imposition and widespread demonstrations were organised. In a radio broadcast in February 1965, Prime Minister Lal Bahadur Shastri promised to honour Nehru's assurances. These assurances and the administration's decision to drop all cases filed against the protest leaders finally led to the end of the protests.

In 1974, Jayprakash Narayan (JP) led the Bihar movement against the State government of Bihar. It became a protest against the central government and Prime Minister Indira Gandhi and he later termed his protest as calling for a *Sampoorna Kranti* (Total Revolution). She imposed Emergency from June 1975 to March 1977. In the elections conducted thereafter, JP led the campaign against Indira Gandhi, and Janata Party became the first non-Congress central government in India.

Narmada Bachao Andolan is a movement (led by respected activist Medha Patkar) against several dams constructed on River Narmada. Members of the movement have held several demonstrations over the years. In this picture, members are conducting a *Jal* (Water) Satyagraha by standing in water for several days together.

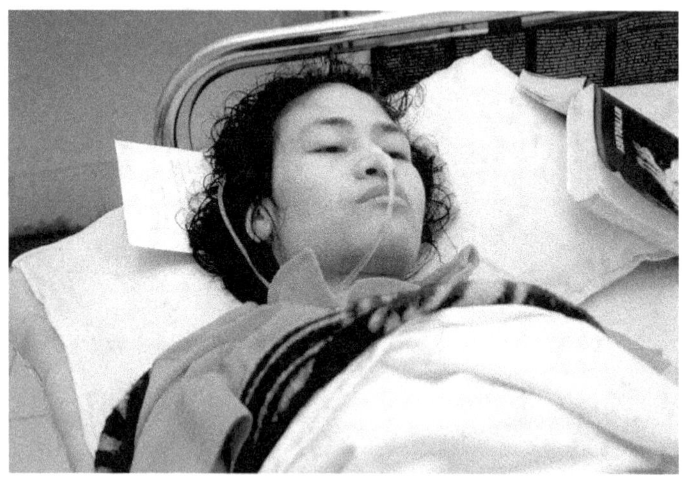

After the massacre of civilians in Malom in the state of Manipur in November 2000, Irom Sharmila went on a hunger strike demanding that the government repeal Armed Forces Special Powers Act (AFSPA). She continued her hunger strike for 16 years, during which the government kept her alive by force-feeding her. United Nations representatives and human rights activists have termed AFSPA as undemocratic. In 2016, the Supreme Court ended the immunity of armed forces from prosecution under AFSPA. But the Act continues to be in force in several parts of North-east India and Jammu & Kashmir.

India's Right to Information Act 2005 owes its origins to years-long demonstrations by Mazdoor Kisan Shakti Sanghathan (founded by Aruna Roy).

India Against Corruption, 2011: In response to a series of corruption allegations, activists under the banner of 'India Against Corruption' conducted several protests against the Congress-led government in the Centre. These protests eventually lead to the electoral victory of Bharatiya Janata Party in the Parliamentary Elections and Aam Aadmi Party in the Delhi assembly elections.

In 2012, thousands protested after a horrific rape incident. In this picture, the police is seen using water cannons on peaceful protesters.

In this picture taken in 2016, Bhopal residents are protesting government's inaction on the company that caused a gas leak in 1984.

Jammu & Kashmir has seen wars, heavy military deployment, peaceful protests, militancy and terror attacks.

• • •

These images show that India has seen a wide range of protests ever since it became Independent.

How should a democratic government react to peaceful protests by its citizens? It should not crush the protest. It should not call the protesters terrorists or anti-nationals. Instead, the government must provide space for dissent, engage protesters in dialogue and try to find an amicable solution within the constitutional framework. That is every government's *dharma* (duty).

CHAPTER V

Conclusion

The Azadi anthem has been widely used across the country to galvanize protesters in 2020. It was reportedly adapted from a feminist anthem against patriarchy. A version of the anthem and its English translation are provided below

Hum kya chahtaein - Azadi!
Zara jor se bolo - Azadi!
Aatankvaad se - Azadi!
Jaativaad se - Azadi!
Manuvaad se - Azadi!
Bhookmari se - Azadi!
Bhedh-bhaav se - Azadi!
Hum lad ke lenge - Azadi!
Tum kuch bhi kar lo - Azadi!
Hum le ke rahenge - Azadi!
Woh haq hamaari - Azadi!
Yeh jaan se pyaari - Azadi!
Hai pyaari pyaari - Azadi!
Gandhi-wali - Azadi!
Phule-wali - Azadi!
Fathima-wali - Azadi!
Bismil-wali - Azadi!
Ambedkar-wali - Azadi!

What do we demand - Freedom!
Say it out aloud - Freedom!
From terror - Freedom!
From casteism - Freedom!

From Manu's philosophy - Freedom!
From starvation - Freedom!
From discrimination - Freedom!
We will fight & get it - Freedom!
Do what you will - Freedom!
But we will definitely get it - Freedom!
It is our right - Freedom!
Love it more than our life - Freedom!
For the love of - Freedom!
Gandhi's dream- Freedom!
Phule's vision - Freedom!
Fathima's vision - Freedom!
Bismil's vision - Freedom!
Ambedkar's vision - Freedom!

The anthem describes the nature of freedom it seeks. It is not to demand secession from the country. It is simply to demand complete freedom for the individual citizen from the problems prevalent in our country.

In a democracy, a government is elected to solve these problems. And when citizens perceive a failure of the government, protest they must.

But do protests solve the problems?

In 2018, a 15-year old girl in Sweden, Greta Thunberg, took to protesting alone every Friday against global inaction on climate change.

And slowly it turned into a global movement. A little over a year later, in September 2019, millions joined her across the globe in a Global Climate Strike. And she said: "I think if enough people get together and stand up for this, then that can have a huge difference, to put pressure on the people in power, to actually hold them accountable and to say you need to do something now".

When you see an injustice or an evil situation arising out of a government's actions or a society's practice, people can force governments to act through peaceful protests. That is a most nationalistic patriotic act of a citizen.

Benjamin Franklin, a Founding Father of USA, alluded to this on the last day of their Constitutional Convention in 1787. He was asked if the USA was going to be a monarchy or a Republic. And he responded: "Republic, if you can keep it".

Every nation is a work in progress and unless citizens remain vigilant, those in power will try to consolidate their power even further and move the country to a dictatorship away from a democratic republic.

And hence, protest we must.